GR8NESS
IN THE MAKING

UNLOCK THE GREATNESS WITHIN

**GR8NESS IN THE MAKING:
UNLOCK THE GREATNESS WITHIN**

ENTERPRISES

**1419 S. Utica
Tulsa, OK 74104
(918)280-8198**

**2018 © Ramona Rogers
Printed in USA
ISBN: 978-1717545473**

To Meggin,
You are a class
act. Keep the
fire. You are destined
for Greatness!!
Tauré
Roggs

3

Foreword

We all face challenges and at times we feel uncertain, but the key is not to allow the challenges to define who you are. The shifts in your life are designed to move you into becoming the most authentic version of yourself. Who you are matters, and transforming your life begins with you. No matter how long you wait, no one is coming to rescue you. Throughout life you've engage in behavior patterns. These patterns influenced your way of thinking, acting and interacting with others. According to Webster a pattern is defined as the regular and repeated way in which something happens or is done. Often without realizing it, we tend to find what works, and then protect and defend it, closing the door to other possibilities.

If this book has found its way to your hands, there is something inside of you that is ready to accept that greatness is a part of your DNA. And it's time to develop the greater person that lives on the inside of you. No worries about where to start, Ramona has brilliantly laid out the Great Eight Strategies. The key is believing in yourself and consistently taking steps toward birthing the greater person inside. Make the commitment to follow them and watch the shift in your patterns and the elevation begin to take place. YOU are GREATNESS IN THE MAKING!

When Ramona Rogers asked me to write the forward for "GR8NESS In The Making", I was honored. I met Ramona over 5 years ago as we were both accomplishing the dream

of becoming certified Life Coaches. During training, she not only acquired coaching skills, but recognized how they applied to her own life as well. Throughout the training she was open and eager to learn, it was clear once she combined the training with her experiences she would make an impact. Over the years, her vision has remained the same, to share her life experiences and skills combined with her passion to be a resource in helping others. It is easy to remain the same, to continue to flow in the same pattern, accepting what is, but Ramona decided to choose otherwise, rising from the ashes over, and over again, discovering the Greatness within and now she is sharing lessons from that journey with us.

Thank you Ramona for your transparency and sometimes painful truth. Continue to be the external force that challenges others to raise their standards, unlocking the greatness within. I am proud of you!

JoAnn Dean, MSW
Certified Life Coach
www.joanndean.com

ACKNOWLEDGEMENTS

I would first like to thank my parents and grandparents for modeling attributes that allowed me to mimic the best parts of them which made me the person I am today.

To my husband Charles, I thank you for your unconditional love and support over the years.

To my daughters Carrington and Cara, raising you made me push past life's disappointments, challenges and obstacles. You were a constant reminder of my purpose in life. Thank you for your love and patience.

To my mother Elaine Watkins, thank you for always supporting me and encouraging me to keep going no matter what. "Fly Bird Fly" were the words that you would always say. Those words would always lift my spirits. Thank you for being my biggest cheerleader.

To my brother Rodney Watkins Jr. You have been my spiritual guide throughout this faith walk. I appreciate all your words of comfort and prayers during my dark times. I was able

to get through many days only because you
were a phone call away.
Thank for being accessible.

To my Coach Joann Dean, thank you for
keeping me on my path to complete this
project.

To my family and friends. All those who
encouraged, supported, talked things over,
read, wrote, offered comments, allowed me to
quote their remarks and even lended their
gifts and talents to help me complete this
book, I am so grateful, and I love you all.

"GREATNESS IS AN INSIDE OUT PROCESS.
YOU FIRST HAVE TO BELIEVE IT'S POSSIBLE. YOU THEN MUST DO ALL THE THINGS THAT WILL MAKE IT POSSIBLE."

RAMONA ROGERS

TABLE OF CONTENTS

INTRODUCTION

We all have the ability to become GREAT. It's not a secret that's set aside for a select few. It's sitting, waiting to be discovered and attained by you, the master of your fate.

Decades of oppression by the powers that be has challenged many to put mundane and mediocrity on notice because they desire to be more and want more out of life. That inner greater person that desired to be birthed, moved, kicked, and maneuvered until Greatness emerged. Time and time again it has been proven that it is attainable by those who really want it.

Discovering Greatness is the road less traveled. Society has tricked its daily participant into believing they only deserve to watch others live life in abundance while they search, worry, and wonder where they will get their next meal.

Society expects and trains the public to live and operate with less than desirable education, wages, and living conditions. The

myth that only special people are worthy of a life style that offers higher education, business ownership, nice homes, cars, extraordinary events, or travel, has crippled the masses to accept a life of mediocrity.

The average working-class citizen believes that life is about struggle and limits. Though many would not admit that's their belief, it can be plainly seen through their actions in their everyday lives. When placed under a microscope, life for many is a cookie cutter repeat of past generations. It's not anyone's fault so to speak. Humans are just creatures of habit. We imitate what we see. We tend to live how our parents and grandparents lived. The same approach to life tends to plague the next generation when you are not taught anything different.

Struggling to survive and waiting for the next hardship is common place to many. Most people are simply a breathing corps just awaiting the date to be added behind the dash on their headstone. That date will indicate the day they took their last breath. The saddest thing is that their life's hopes and dreams are

buried long before the individual physically dies.

I wrote this book because I grew tired of seeing so much hopelessness and mediocrity in the world. The worst part about it is that the people in the most devastating situations, seemed to be okay with just being given what someone deemed was a sufficient supply or adequate resource.

That has always been so unsettling for me. I was never the type to wait around until someone decided to give me something. I always had an excellent work ethic. I learned this from my parents and grandparents. My dad, the late Rodney L. Watkins Sr., always said, "There are 24 hours in a day, go make your own money so you don't have to wait on anyone to give you anything."

Those words have boosted me many times throughout my life. Throughout the years I've experienced my own struggles of learning and developing the greater person inside.   That greater person emerged on June 21, 2017 and everything finally made sense.

My life experiences and skills combined with my passion to be a resource to help others find their Greatness, gave me a new calling. GR8NESS IN THE MAKING was born.

That day I decided to dedicate my life to the "Greatness Movement". With that mindset I pinned these words, "I finally accepted the fact that it is my job and responsibility to inspire and empower others to Unlock their GREATNESS".

In the pages to come I have outlined how you too can discover your GREATNESS.

The formula to GREATNESS must be incorporated into your everyday life.

You must first accept that GREATNESS is a part of your DNA and then spend every moment developing the great person that lives inside of you. It's not an easy task, but it can be attained if you practice the Great Eight Strategies outlined in this book.

We can look at past and present individuals from all spectrums of life who decided to unlock their GREATNESS.

Some easily identifiable individuals would be:

Abraham Lincoln	Jimmie Hendricks
The Wright Brothers	Muhammad Ali
George Washington	Ray Charles
Beethoven	Will Smith
Thomas Edison	Bruno Mars
Picasso	Barack Obama
Steven Jobs	Russell Westbrook
Bill Gates	Serena Williams
Michael Jackson	Venus Williams
Michael Jordan	Damion John
Matt Damon	Phil Knight
Elton John	Lori Greiner

The list goes on and on. These individuals carried out the GREAT formula which allowed their gifts and talents to elevate them into their GREATNESS.

Brendon Birchers, author of *The Motivation Manifesto*, says it like this, "we must dedicate ourselves to self-mastery; we must determine

and discipline our own motivations to stay true to our own sense of self, to our own path."

It's that thought process that has challenged me to set in motion a movement for unlocking GREATNESS.

This is attainable for anyone who is willing to follow the GREAT Eight Formula and implement it into every area of your life. You must believe in yourself, develop your knowledge, skills, gifts, and talents. Most of all, you must take action every day towards birthing the greater person inside.

Believe, Develop, and Take Action.

You are GREATNESS In The Making.

It's a journey worth taking, and it will be the road less traveled. Only the determined and committed individual that desires to become the person you were born to be should continue reading.

If this is what you seek out of life, I applaud you and welcome you to your journey of unlocking the greatness within.

The Significance of the number 8 in the GR8NESS Formula:

The number 8 has many meanings and interpretations. For the sake of this book we will focus on the fact that in the Bible the number 8 signifies Resurrection and Regeneration. It is the number of new beginnings. Eight is also associated with the beginning of a new era or that of a new order.

Since you decided to take the journey to reach your greatness level, the number 8 will serve to remind you of your new destination. While on your Greatness journey you will need to stay focused on your daily goals.

The number 8 will also serve to remind you to maintain harmony, peace and balance in your life while you implement the 8 elements of the Greatness Formula.

Made in the Image of GREATNES

The focus of the Greatness journey is to become the person you were created to be. In order to grasp that concept, it is important for you to understand who the creator is.

The Creator is the embodiment of Greatness. He is the benchmark and the standard. Because we as humans are made in the image and the likeness of our Creator, we too have the ability to become Great.

It's not enough just to know that you have the ability to become Great, you also have to have a Why?

Your Why has to be a part of your Greatness journey.

Your Why has to be so compelling that you would do whatever it takes in order to get the outcome that you desire.

Your Why will be your fuel for your Greatness journey. Refuel as often as you needed.

Remind yourself daily of why you are in pursuit of your goals, hopes and dreams.

Your Why will be the element that keeps you going during your process towards Greatness.

VISION

"Create the highest Grandest vision possible for your life, because you become what you believe" ~ Oprah Winfrey

In order for anything to be accomplished in life, it always has to start with a dream or idea of what is to be. This concept is called Vision.

Having a vision about where you want to go in life is essential to the process of achieving Greatness. Vision is the key to unlocking the Greatness within.

Without A Vision for your life, you waste a lot of valuable time going nowhere.

Without vision you cannot put in place the goals and action steps that are required for your roadmap of your life's accomplishments.

Vision pinpoints the outcome you want. The Greatness formula is the process that will allow you to plan and apply the process daily so that your Greatness will emerge.

Here are a few questions that will get you started towards your vision design.

- Who are you?
- What attributes or qualities do you have?
- What are your hopes and dreams?
- What do you want your life to look like?

Knowing who you are, your attributes, gifts and talents, has a direct effect on your ability to accept the fact that you were born to be GREAT.

Most people laugh at the notion that they can have the word GREAT associated with them.

I too was once that person, but over the years I have learned what it takes to operate at a level that allows me to reach my potential and become the GREAT person I was created to be.

Until you can answer these questions thoroughly, the Greatness process cannot be practiced. An unobstructed vision of the desired outcome must be in place.

When you can answer the above questions and you have an idea of what you want your life to look like, you can proceed to the next chapter where you will start to learn the process of Greatness.

THE WORD SAYS:

> **Write down the revelation and make it plain on tablets so that a herald may run with it. For the revelation awaits an appointed time; it speaks of the end and will not prove false. Though it lingers, wait for it; it will certainly come and will not delay.**
> **Habakkuk 2:2-3**

GOALS

"Setting goals is the first step to creating a life that you can live with purpose and on purpose."
~ Ramona Rogers

Operating in a way that provides advancements and rewards has eluded many for generations. It's almost cliché to advise people to set goals in life.

In order to get anywhere, be it geographically or advancement, there has to be some kind of directive in place or road map? The purpose of these tools is to help individuals get to their desired result or destination.

Why do so many people live their life without creating a road map? That's all goal setting is. A possible result or outcome. The truth of the matter is they have not been taught or never learned that the key to advancement and achievement is simply having goals that you want to reach and then taking the necessary steps to achieve those goals or desired results.

Most people do it every day without realizing it. All the responsibilities a person has on a day to day bases causes them to set daily goals to take care of their responsibilities. Something as simple as getting to work on time requires setting a goal and taking the necessary actions to achieve the goal of getting to work on time. On the surface most people are just doing a daily routine, but when you stop and analyze the actual thought process of fulfilling the task of daily routines, you will find that the skill of goal setting is a part of our daily lives. It's only when you ask people about their hopes and dreams and what are their life goals, that they feel overwhelmed and discount goal setting as a vital part of their existence or an avenue to reach their hopes and dreams.

You've probably heard the phrase " if you fail to plan, you plan to fail", numerous times during your life. The phrase is simple, yet most people ignore the message. They live life as if it were a game of Russian Roulette. Instead of a bullet being the object that ends a life, failure is the critical component that kills the spirit of GREATNESS.

Failure in life is simply the byproduct of not having a plan in place to live by.
A plan is simply a goal. If individuals don't make a goal to live their life by, the Greatness that lives within will never be able to emerge. So, the first strategy in allowing your GREATNESS to emerge is Goal Setting.

Goal setting should be implemented for every area of your life. Family, education, health, career, and your finances all require their own individual plan for you to maintain balance and progression throughout your life.

As you approach the task of setting goals for various areas of your life, you must use a method that will help you gauge whether your goals will get you your desired result. I encourage you to use the SMART approach.
SMART GOALS

Smart goals can help you during the goal setting process. SMART can stand for several things, but I like to use the following:

S- Specific
M-Measurable
A-Attainable
R-Realistic
T-Timely

Applying the SMART approach to Short Term and Long-Term goals for every area of your life will assist you with setting goals that can be reached by actively pursuing your goals daily and taking the necessary actions that will help the goal become reality. Short Term goals should be set for 30 days, 60 days, 90 days, 1 year, and 2 years. Long term goals should be set for 5 years, and 10 years.

Goal setting is a part of every successful person's daily routine. Those individuals that we see on various media outlets or the big screen, have mastered the first strategy of GREATNESS. They set SMART GOALS and take the necessary actions to reach their goals which sets their GREATNESS (persona) into action.

Goal Setting can be a little uncomfortable when you first begin. To help you get started I

have provided an outline for you to follow in the supplemental section. Simply use the outline for each area of your life.
(Example: Spiritual, Relationships, Education, Career, Health, Finances)

The Words Says:

**The plans of the diligent leads to profit, as surely as haste leads to poverty.
Proverbs 21:5**

Goal Setting Activity

In this chapter I introduced you to the first strategy in the Greatness formula. Goals

In order to start the journey to Greatness, there are several questions you have to answer to provide a foundation to base your goals on. Take some time to really think about the question before you answer.

List 3 attributes that describe you.

What are your interest?

What are your hobbies?

What are your strengths?

What are your weaknesses?

What are your hopes and dreams?

What vision do you have for your life?

Where do you want to see yourself in 5 years?

Write down 3 goals you want to accomplish within 12 months

Once you have completed the list of questions on the previous page, you can now create what I call **"Your Life Blueprint."**

A Life Blueprint is simple a visual guide you create that will allow you to map out what you want your life to look like and the steps to take in order for you to reach each goal. Basically, you are making a schedule of what you want to happen in your life. Intentional activity.

We are going to work backwards to create a blueprint to achieve your goals.
*the following list should be done on separate sheets of paper.

- Make a list of 3 goals you want to accomplish in 30 days.

- Make a list of 3 goals you want to accomplish in 60 days.

- Make a list of 3 goals you want to accomplish in 90 days.

- Make a list of 3 goals you want to accomplish in 1 year.

RESILIENCE

"Life doesn't get easier or more forgiving, we just get stronger and more resilient."
- Unknown

Life is filled with uncertainties. The only thing that is certain in life is the fact that the element of change is sure to affect every aspect of your life time and time again. Changes that affect life will come in the form of setbacks, heartache, heartbreak, let downs, disappointment, mishaps, mis-steps, challenges, circumstances, and obstacles.

As I'm writing this chapter I am recalling many changes that came in the various forms of what I mentioned in the above sentence. Changes don't announce when they will arrive. Subconsciously we all know changes will happen in our lives, but when they occur, we are never prepared to handle them. They seem to show up at the worst possible times and catch us off guard.

So, the question then becomes, what do you do or how do you handle the changes when they come?

There is an attribute that you must embody to deal with the changing seasons in your life. That attribute is called RESILIENCE.

Resilience is defined as the ability to adapt and overcome. It's mostly referred to as the fight within.

To give you a clearer picture of what resilience is, here's an illustration. Go find a rubber band. Now stretch it as many times as you want. Regardless of how far or how many times you stretch the rubber band; it returns to its original shape. The rubber band is pliable and flexible. Humans are designed the same way.

Throughout the process of change you must be able to be flexible when you are stretched out of your comfort zone, when your life gets altered, or when something in your life is drastically changed. You end up in a place that you never thought was possible. You're

forced to create and embrace a new normal. The process is repeated throughout the course of your life. You exercise resilience when the winds of life force you to recreate, reinvent or reposition yourself. Your ability to adapt and overcome allows you to build your resilience gene.

Sometimes it will feel like life has gotten the best of you. It is during those times when that thing that lies deep within forces you to muster up enough strength to bounce back after life has dealt a blow that was so severe it would cause you to give up on life. The resilience gene should help you cope with your season of unrest. It should sustain you while you recover from the changes that occur.

Resilience is referred to as the thing that helps you fight every element that tries to inhibit your ability to survive.

I can recall a time when my business wasn't going very well. I had done all that I knew to do and tapped in to every resource I had in order to get my preschool to operate efficiently and become profitable. It seemed like

everything I tried could not elevate my business to get over the hump. I even had to go out and work another job just to give money to my business, so it could stay afloat. A friend of mine called me one day during that period, he could sense something was wrong and began to ask me what was going on with me and the business. I told him how I felt like I was being punched in the face and it seemed like every avenue I tried to maneuver, I kept hitting a dead end and I even uttered the words, I'm tired of feeling like I've been beat up.! After allowing me to vent for a few moments, he responded with these words, **"NEVER LOSE YOUR FIGHT."**

Those word were like music to me. It was almost like he gave me permission to use my resilience gene. I devoted intentional activities towards turning the situation around. I even surprised myself with some of the ideas I came up with and the new energy of making this situation turn in my favor. It was one of the hardest things I've ever done, but it was also one of the most rewarding experiences because it helped me to build my resilience gene.

There will be numerous times and opportunities when you get to practice resilience.

Resilience also must be displayed when you try something new.
Moving outside of your comfort zone and learning new skills and acquiring new knowledge brings about growth and an elevated version of yourself. Because there is a process of change that will take place with the new thing in your life, there will be a certain degree of resilience that you will have to apply while you are going through the learning process.

Your ability to adapt to the many changes that should occur when you learn something new will help you develop resilience.

In order to hone the resilience gene, you must lay the foundation by deciding you will overcome any obstacle that comes your way.

By displaying resilience during a season of change, it will propel you to your next level of life.

You should gain strength during the rough times and grow during your season of struggle. A life without pain and struggle is a life without growth. Pain makes you elevate your game.

You can't plan for all of life's minor changes, but you can always be ready to adjust to something. Everything happens for a reason. Some things are known immediately while others are revealed over a period time as to the role it played towards you reaching your level of Greatness.

Great people adjust when obstacles or challenges present themselves. They don't make excuses or retreat. Stand your ground. Stay focus and on course. It's all a part of the GREATNESS process.

The Word Says:

> **"Have I not commanded you? Be strong and courageous. Do not be terrified; do not be discouraged, for the Lord your God will be with you wherever you go."**
> **Joshua 1:9**

Resilience Activity

In Chapter Two, I introduced the attribute of resilience and talked about its importance in your journey towards Greatness.

In this exercise I want you to recall a time or situation when you had to display resilience.

- How did it make you feel?

- What did you learn from the experience?

- How did the situation help you grow?

EFFORT

"Anyone can be great when they first decide that's what they want to be and make a daily commitment to put forth the effort to do whatever it takes for their greatness to evolve."
~Ramona Rogers

This chapter was very difficult for me to write because I was trying to think of the simplest way to explain what effort means and how it should be applied to you in your journey to unlocking your Greatness.

I thought of all the effort I put in to every aspect of my daily life and I came up with 6 elements that would help me illustrate the importance of effort and the role it plays in the GR8NESS formula.

E -Exhaustion
F- Force-power or influence
F- Fortitude -courage in the mist of pain and adversity
O- Obligation- committed

R- Resistance-your ability not to be impacted by something
T- Tenacity -persistence, determination

All day, every day, with everything I do, I give it all I got until the task is completed. I make a conscious effort to go above and beyond. I learned this habit by watching my parents raise 9 children. By having a work ethic that requires me to be thorough, it sometimes leaves me exhausted. With that being said, if you put forth an effort with anything you do, exertion will be the result. Quite frankly, if you aren't exhausted daily, chances are, you haven't put forth as much effort as you should. Exertion is a part of the process.

My current position in the airline industry sometimes requires that I work extra hours when weather events cause extra airplanes and people to land at my station. I've worked 22 hours before, went home and slept for two hours so that I could return to work to process planes and people out of the station the next morning. Of course, I was totally exhausted, but I was willing to do whatever was required to complete any task that would allow planes

and people to resume their day after the weather event had disrupted life for everyone.

Exhaustion should also be experienced when you make the effort to advance your skills and knowledge. In order for your Greatness to emerge, you will constantly have to add new layers or skill and knowledge to your Greatness gene. This must be done in addition to you working a full-time job and raising children.

I can recall a time when I was running a child care facility and decided that I needed to learn more about best practices of being a child care provider. I already had a Bachelor's Degree in another field, but I needed to learn about the space that I was in at that time. An Associate Degree in Early Childhood Education became my focus. Going to school would be in addition to running a business and meeting the needs of my husband and two children who were ages 2 and 5 months. I had 39 credit hours I needed to complete in order to get the Associates Degree.

The first 2 semesters I took 2 classes which were 3 credit hours for each class. After 9 months I only had 12 hours completed which meant it was going to take me several years to complete the requirements for the Associates Degree I was seeking. So, I decided to make the effort and complete all the classes within a year. That meant I would be in school full time for two semesters. Five classes giving me 15 credit hours for one semester then finishing the remaining 12 hours and 3 internships the second semester.

That was a very challenging 9 month, but I knew my efforts would get me the results I wanted. I had to maintain my business, my family and my school work throughout the whole time. I graduated with a 3.5 Grade Point Average.

The second element of effort is Force. There will be many time when you simply don't want to make an effort to do anything towards the discovery of your Greatness. It is during these times that you must force yourself to make the effort to do the things you need to do. Force is simply having the power to decide you are

going to make an effort regardless of how you feel or what situations may come up during the day. You must muster up enough strength to force yourself to take the necessary action daily so the results you want to see will manifest.

The third element of effort is Fortitude. During your daily efforts to operate at the Greatness level, you must display an elevated level of fortitude.

Fortitude is simply having courage in the mist of pain or adversity. Regardless of what path you choose, pain and adversity will come. That's just a fact of life. The truth of the matter is the more you focus your sights on achieving your goals, hopes and dreams, adversity is sure to rear its ugly head. Many times, when pain and adversity come along, most people are easily discouraged from moving towards their target. Instead they retreat and give way to the life circumstance or situation that has reared his head. It is during these times the attribute of fortitude must be exhibited. Effort must be a part of your daily practice as a seeker to operate at a level of Greatness.

The fourth element of effort is Obligation. Obligation in this sense is simply making a commitment to yourself to take the necessary actions that will mold you and push you to think and act on a level that sets you apart. When you make a commitment to yourself, you must hold yourself accountable to take inventory of the people, places and things that you allow to live in your space and influence you. You are obligated to surround yourself with those things that will help you make the effort to reach your destination of operating at a level of Greatness in every facet of your life.

The fifth element of effort is Resistance. The refusal to accept or comply with the obstacles that will try to deter you from your pursuit of honing your Greatness skills will occur on a regular basis. It will seem like the obstacles are insurmountable at times, but you must resist the temptation to give up and make the decision and the effort to overcome obstacles. Learning to cope with adversity builds your confidence and over a period of time you will develop a strategy that will allow you to conquer obstacles which will advance you towards operating at your level of Greatness.

The sixth and final element of my effort illustration is Tenacity. Tenacity is having the determination to go after what you want in life. Most people relate tenacity to athletes but being tenacious should definitely be applied in the journey of reaching your level of Greatness.

One of the first things that come to mind when I think of the attribute of tenacity is the fact that there first must be the belief that you can become the great person you were created to be. The tenacity and determination you possess will be evident by how you as a person excel at each stage of your Greatness journey. You must have a can't stop, won't stop approach to defeat the challenges that will come. You will have to stay focused while you are in pursuit of reaching your level of Greatness. You must be determined, no matter what, to reach your goal of Greatness.

Desired results is a combination of a lot of effort put into action over a period of time. It is an individual choice to put forth a great amount of effort on a daily basis in order to operate at a level if Greatness.

You get out of life what you put into it. If you aren't where you want to be in any area, chances are the results of what you are seeing and experiencing are associated with the effort you put forth on a daily basis.

The reward of effort is an innate feeling that can only be experienced by the person who puts forth the effort. Your degree of effort can only be measured by the outcome of what you are seeking.

Effort will beat out talent every time. You can have all the talent in the world, but if you don't put forth an effort to sharpen your talent by building your skills, the talent is then wasted.

Effort is only beneficial when you give 100% of it daily in order for the great person that lives within to emerge.

The Words Says:

Whatever your hand finds to do, do it with all your might, for in the grave, where you are going, there is neither working nor planning nor knowledge nor wisdom.
Ecclesiastes 9:10

Effort Assessment

To gauge your current level when it comes to effort, answer the following questions.

1. When you really want something, do you make every effort to make sure you get your desired result?

2. Do you wait for others to make things happen for you?

3. Do you put forth extra effort towards things that are difficult?

4. Can you recall a time when you wished you would have made the effort to do more to get the result you wanted?

These questions are meant to simply give you a glimpse of your past actions. By reflecting on what you have done the past, will allow you to see that your level of effort will have to change in order for you to experience the outcomes that you want.

ATTITUDE

"Attitude is a little thing that makes a significant difference."
- Unknown

Growing up, I was oblivious to the fact that my attitude would be one of the key elements that would help me become successful if it was positive, and if it were negative, it would yield me to live a disappointing and mediocre life.

Attitude is an innate element that can be seen at its best or worst when you experience obstacles and challenges in life.
You hear it time and time again as you are growing up that you should have a positive attitude. In my opinion, because attitude is an internal element, most people fail to grasp the concept of its importance and they have not been given a clear definition of what it is and the role it plays in life.

Because I know it's a key element on the road to unlocking your greatness, I will give you a clear definition that you can understand and apply to your day to day life.

Attitude is simply the way you approach anything going in.

Attitude comes from your expectations of outcomes. Expectations come from your belief and values. Your attitudes do not form overnight but are developed over the course of your life.

The outcome of your experiences has a lot to do with whether you have a positive or negative attitude. Life situations should not be the determining factor as to what attitude you embody.

The truth of the matter is that many people exist in and survive in less than ideal living situations, but the key to their survival is the belief that the situation will one day get better, and the positive attitude to keep going.

Having a positive attitude has been the one element that has helped me throughout my various stages of life.

When tough times or difficult situations arose, I always maintained my appearance and

acted as if everything was fine. I subscribe to the philosophy of acting the part. Even though I was an emotional wreck, I looked at these situations as necessary life events to give me opportunities to redo, revamp, recreate or simply move in a different direction. My positive attitude towards my life events allowed me to have a never give up mentality which sustained me until things changed.

One of the most overlooked elements of personal advancement is the role attitude plays. Your attitude determines your altitude meaning your success or failure will be determined by your attitude.

Throughout the Greatness process there will be days when you will want to give up because the task or skill at hand will seem like it's impossible to master. It's during those times that if your attitude remains positive, it will get you through the tough times. If negativity resides, it allows for doubt and defeat to step in.

You must embody a never give up attitude in order to view your mistakes, missteps and

failures as an opportunity to try it again a different way or with a different focus.

When you have the attitude of never giving up or never stopping, it allows you to grow through your process of mastering your present skill. If you succeeded the first, second or third time, you don't get to sharpen your approach or push yourself to pull all that is within you, to get past that point.

Throughout the Greatness process you will face challenges and obstacles that you absolutely hate and would prefer not to do. That is when you will need the attitude and understanding that the Greatness process will take you down some roads that will seem impossible to overcome. It is through this process that your Greatness muscles will be built.

Unfortunately having a negative attitude is a normal element of life that will rob you of your existence. In order for you to reach your Greatness level, you will have to learn how to manage your negative natural attitude. You must adopt the never give up attitude. When

you do, you will be able to proceed through the Greatness process with a better focus and understanding of how to approach your next challenge.

A part of the never say die attitude is the belief that you have in yourself and your ability to overcome any challenging task or obstacle that you face on your journey towards Greatness.

Here's something to keep in mind:

- ✓ Great Attitude = Great Results
- ✓ Good Attitude = Good Results
- ✓ Average Attitude = Average Results
- ✓ Poor Attitude = Poor Results

A positive attitude tends to produce much more favorable results. You must decide daily what attitude you will take towards your current situation. The journey towards your Greatness will test and entice you daily. In order for your Greatness to emerge, make the wise choice to have a positive attitude every day towards everything.

The Word Says:

And have put on the new self, which is being renewed in knowledge in the image of the Creator.

Colossians 3:10

Attitude Activity

In order to move towards operating at a level of Greatness, we need to pause here to assess your attitude and outlook of life situations and changes.

1. When unexpected situations occur, how do you handle them?
2. Do you tend to avoid situations or experiences that will cause a major shift in your life?
3. How do you feel when changes occur in your life?
4. Do you blame others when the results you desire are not achieved?
5. How do you approach a difficult situation?

There is no right or wrong answer to the above questions. This activity is strictly for you to reflect on your thoughts, feelings and attitude about where you are presently in these areas.

The goal is to learn to view life and all its elements in a positive manner regardless of the negative or hopeless undertone.
Your attitude can be an asset for you if it's positive or a liability that will not allow you to make the Greatness process progressive.

TEACHABLE/TRAINABLE

"Being teachable and trainable is essential for growth in every area of your life."
~ Ramona Rogers

Being able to learn from the people that have done what you want to do. You don't always have to figure it out on your own or re-invent the wheel.

You must develop a coachable and teachable mindset.

Your inability to learn from others will derail the Greatness process.

Being teachable means you are willing to change so you can transform and excel. With this mindset you understand that you don't have all the answers. It's crucial for you to surround yourself with others that have the wisdom, knowledge, and experience to get you where you are trying to go.

Being teachable is going to make you feel vulnerable and uncomfortable. Being able to

go through this stage throughout your process of unlocking your Greatness, is the key element that allows your Greatness to emerge.

Emergence of Greatness will be halted if you are the kind of person that always has to be right. The process of being teachable will be difficult for you if you think you are your best teacher. If you aren't willing to change old habits and replace them with new ones, this process will be impossible for you to master

Always looking at things negative or making negative comments will also cause the Greatness process to derail.

You MUST be able to self-reflect and not blame others for where you are. You must be willing to grow. In order for growth to occur, you have to embrace the fact that change will be a constant and necessary component of the teachable process.

Other elements that are a part of the teachable process is you must be open, receptive, and make any obstacle in life seem

doable. Throughout the process you will become an inspiration to others because they will see the results of your growth and your willingness to be teachable.

Have an action bias of doing whatever it takes to get past something that is difficult or challenging. You have to be hungry to become the greater you.

Benefits of the teachable aspect is knowing that the desired result is only going to happen after you go through the process of being taught and adopting the mindset, habits and wisdom to allow your Greatness to emerge.

You must be able to use feedback to improve. You should take advantage of every opportunity to keep getting better. Weekends and holidays don't give you a pass to bypass your process. Being able to break away from normal daily routines and obligations should prompt you to devote your time and energy towards your Greatness development.

You must be committed to switching to what's uncomfortable long enough to allow your new

knowledge and habits to become comfortable. The danger in not being teachable is the fact that you don't know what you don't know.

A big factor in the teachable process is you have to be able to receive and implement instructions. The result of not being teachable will be no implementation of new knowledge or opportunities to grow you. This means there can be no progression towards your ultimate goal.

Be prepared to listen and learn from others at every stage of your Greatness journey.

The Word Says:

> **Instruct a wise man and he will be wiser still; teach a righteous man and he will add to his learning.**
>
> **Proverbs 9:9**

Teachable/Trainable Activity

You have just read the chapter over the teachable component of The GR8NESS process.

Now answer the following questions to gauge your outlook on being teachable.

1. Do you listen with an open mind?

2. Do you welcome feedback when it pushes you out of your comfort zone?

3. Are you open to changing habits if you are advised to?

4. Do you take responsibility for your results?

NAVIGATE

"The road to success is not easy. You must work hard, be determined and have passion to navigate to your greatness destination."
~ Ramona Rogers

Congratulations, YOU have made it to the Sixth component of The GR8NESS Process!

When you saw the word Navigate at the top of this page, I'm sure your first thought was what does navigate have to do with bringing out the greatness within? Unfortunately, this is an element of life that detours many well intended individuals off the path of becoming the GREAT person they were born to be.

The definition of the word navigate is to plan and direct the route or course of something. In this book, the route I am referring to is your life's journey. Just as a road trip to any destination can encounter detours and roadblocks that make you alter your original routing, the same concept happens in life.

These days, most people can't find a location without using a GPS. GPS stands for Global Positioning System which is a device that is intended to help the user take the best route to their destination. This tool is not always accurate and when it does fail, the user is forced to use an alternate directional tool. The same philosophy applies when life happens to an individual. When your original routing is interrupted by mistakes, mishaps or strategy, your navigational tool must be updated or changed. You must be willing to invest in a new tool whether it's new knowledge, new surroundings, new processes or new people that will aid you in rerouting your life's course.

On the road to greatness a big part of navigating is knowing that there are going to be ups and downs in life. What matters the most is what you do when those ups and downs occur. When certain things happen in life, you must reflect on them and make a decision to learn something from the situation and use that new information for you next season of life.

The way you respond to life or what happens in life is key to being able to back up and regroup so you can restart your journey. As long as you can breathe there should be nothing that comes your way that will stop you for becoming the best version of yourself and your commitment to pursue your goals, hopes and dreams come what may.

No season or situation lasts forever. All situations, mistakes, mishaps and obstacles give way to the element of implementing your navigational skills to rethink, revise, restructure or reshape your life's plan and the actions that you need to take to stay on your road to Greatness path. If you have been operating without a life plan and you are at a crossroad and you don't know how to proceed, following The GR8NESS Formula will be the tool that can give you the blueprint that you need to propel you forward towards your next season of life.

I've been mentoring and coaching individuals for several years and most will attest that their biggest obstacles are being able to navigate their life when things don't go as planned. I

thought it would be helpful to you, the reader of this book, if I shared responses to these two questions:

1. What does navigating life mean to you?
2. How do you navigate life?

Being able to flow in life and being able to adjust when there is a detour in that planned flow. Actively living life and not passively existing. ~ Rodria Golden

Navigating life has a different meaning for the different seasons of my life. As I evolved the meaning has too.

20s- meant getting through all the goals going to college finishing- getting a job - getting the car I wanted- The navigation meant more visible goals...and completing them. More of a time of being self-absorbed

30s- navigating was more about getting to the happily ever after with mate- kids- job in the field. Start living...that began to change at the end of 30s began to want to be my best self and explored what that looked like

40s -was more about me enjoying the journey being present right now and not getting caught up in planning life instead of living life...understanding what's my truth and being ok...letting go and being open to new things! Not being caught up with superficial aesthetics of people but search for deeper friendships and relationships. ~Ronica Watkins Assistant Budget Officer, Entrepreneur, PH.D (ABD)

Navigating life ......I've learned change will happen whether we are prepared for it or not. Our role is to nurture our mind, body and most importantly our spirit. I believe my steps are ordered by God and time with Him gives me wisdom for the journey and the ability to accept life as it unfolds. Life is filled with lessons and blessings! ~ Joann Dean, Author, Life Coach

Having goals, ambitions and knowing what you need to get there. ~Tracy White-Davidson, Accountant

To map things out, plan ahead, and stick to your plan. Work around the problems and keep going. ~ Cara Rogers Age 15

My life, and the ministry I live is to show someone simply that:

"God has more for your life "

I help people navigate life by recognizing that no matter where they're at, in a season of plenty or a season of need, always walk in an awareness that God Has More for Your Life. Sometimes we get stuck on reaching a specific destination and don't realize that this specific destination is just a stop along the journey. Always realizing that God has more for your life will equip a person with humbly submitting themselves to a life that is continually in pursuit of Glorifying God in all they do.~Rodney Watkins Jr. Minister, Financial Advisor

As you can see from the responses, being able to navigate life will be a continuous action on your road to Greatness. I encourage you to embrace it and understand that being able to

navigate is simply part of the journey to unlocking your Greatness.

The Word Says:

> **Consider it pure joy, my brothers, whenever you face trials of many kinds, because you know that the testing of your faith develops perseverance. Perseverance must finish its work so that you may be mature and complete, not lacking anything.**
> **James 1:2-4**

EXECUTE

*"Goals are useless unless you execute a plan
that will make them become a reality."*
-Ramona Rogers

Growing up my family occasionally took road
trips to visit my grandparents which was a
four-hour drive. On the drive we occasionally
passed by a cemetery or two. I have seven
siblings so to break up the monotony of the
long drive, my father would ask as we passed
by a cemetery, how many people do you think
are dead in that cemetery? As you can
imagine with eight kids in the car, there were
various guesses. None of which were ever
the correct answer. My father would
eventually reveal the answer which was, all of
them. He would then say, "The grave yard is
the richest place on earth". Of course, with
eight kids in the car someone would always
ask, "Why do you say that?" He would go on
to explain that many people that are dead had
great ideas, hopes and dreams, but because
they never made a plan and executed their
idea, it went to the grave with them.

I never forgot that story and I never understood it until I became an adult.
He passed in 2002. Unfortunately, he joined the ranks of the rich once he died. The rich meaning the ideas, hopes and dreams that he had were buried with him too. He was never able to execute what he wanted to come to fruition. I now refer to graveyards as "Greatness In the Ground" My father's inability to execute his ideas has inspired me to learn the process of planning and executing which is essential to the journey towards Greatness. I share this because I don't want anyone joining the ranks of the rich after they have taken their last breath.

The Definition of Execute is the carrying out or putting into effect a plan, order or a course of action.

Before you can execute, you must have a plan. It's great to have a plan in place that will give you a layout or blueprint on what needs to be done to get the finished product or desired result. It doesn't matter if you have a plan in place if you fail to execute it.

Execution simply means taking action.

In order to carry out any plan, you have to be committed and disciplined to do the necessary things regardless of how you may feel or whatever else may come up in your day.

The element of execution, putting action towards your plan, will allow your ideas, goals, hopes and dreams to reach and exceed the desired results.

You must put in the time and effort and do the work to execute your goals hopes and dreams of reaching your Greatness potential. Being hungry to achieve your goals is part of the execution process. If you don't put the time in and make sacrifices with your time, energy and activities, chances are, you Greatness journey will get derailed. All your daily actions and activities should be intentional towards your desired result.

Greatness is a journey, so your mindset should be to make a plan and then work the plan. Repeat this action every day. If this is not working, create another plan and start the

process of doing something every day towards attaining your desired result.

For best results, it will require constant attention and massive action. We aren't just talking about accomplishing one goal and then you are done with the process, we are talking about bringing out your greatness which is going to have to be a new kind of lifestyle for anyone that hopes to reach their Greatness level.

Here are some ways to help you Execute your daily goals and plans. Adopt these habits to master the element of execution.

It's all about ACTION!

A - Allocate adequate amount of time to master a new skill or learn new knowledge

C- Commit to the process and do something every day that will move you towards a new level of understanding or skill set.

T- Tenacious towards obstacles. You must be unwavering, untiring and unshakable. Challenges and obstacles will rear their ugly heads, but you must stay the course and demonstrate self-discipline to help you overcome.

I- Implement the necessary people and processes that will help you make daily progress towards your desired result.

O- Observe and Evaluate any area that seems to prevent you from progressing towards mastering the level or phases you are at.

N- Never Give Up. The Greatness Journey is not for the faint at heart. It's for those that

believe they were born to be Great and are willing to do whatever it takes to unlock it and let it live.

The Word Says:

Many are the plans in a man's heart, but it is the Lord's purpose that prevails.   **Proverbs 19:21**

A more Tangible way to assist you in your execution efforts is to create guidelines and deadlines on a 30-day calendar. This will help you to see what you are doing and hold yourself accountable to make sure the items on your calendar get done.

Feel free to incorporate whatever tool you need to measure you progress.

Plan your work then work your plan!

I have created a calendar for you to use that can be found in the Supplemental section of this book. **GR8NESS IN THE MAKING 30 Day Calendar.**

STANDARDS

"The quality of GREATNESS is reflected in the high-standards a person sets for themselves."
~Ramona Rogers

Throughout my life I often heard the word standards, but I never really paid attention to how standards played a significant role in the way I function as a person.

Growing up in a household of ten had its challenges with meeting the daily needs of all the family members, but my mother set a standard that promoted structure, orderliness, cleanliness and discipline. You could not tell there were eight children living in my mother's house because of the standards she set.

My family didn't have a lot of money, but the standards my parents set allowed me and my siblings to pattern our lives in a way that would set us apart from others.

I remember having glass coffee tables and an all glass screen door in my mother's living

room that I was responsible for cleaning daily. The morning sun that shone into the living room of the home reveled streaks or areas that I might have missed.

My mother was not very forgiving if she had to point out something you missed while attending to your chores. There were consequences, but the outcome was that I mastered cleaning my mother's glass furniture and now every time I go to a public establishment and the glass on the front door is not cleaned, I find the manager and let them know their front doors needs some attention. I share with the store manager that their front door is the first impression that you give to the customers. I further explain that first impressions are lasting impressions. I try to be an external force that raises the cautiousness and standards for the store managers.

On the journey to achieve Greatness, the only force that you will have to contend with is the force from within. No outside force can set the standards that you will have to adopt in order to operate at your Greatness level.

To set yourself apart you have to raise your standards. People should know you by your work ethic and the standards you set.

Standards is something you live, breath and try to get to no matter what. Whenever an obstacle or situation threatens to interrupt or sabotage your plans, your standards should aid you in finding a way to get past or get through anything.

Raising your standards is essential to who you are trying to become. You will have to **Identify** yourself in a new way.   Only the GREAT live by a standard that is unlike that of the majority of the population. You must create a culture of going above and beyond. That should **Become** your new normal.

Raising your standards will be a lasting change element on your road to Greatness. Changing for the better, mastering new skills, gaining new knowledge, and conquering obstacles will be life in the GREATNESS spectrum.

All day every day you know there are things that you should do to raise your standards, but for some reason you have only been consistent with knowing what you should do, but not doing anything at all. Tony Robbins puts like this, "you have to turn your should into your must and you should raise the standards of what you expect from yourself." The must do items that get completed on a day to day bases will be the fuel you need to continue to raise the bar for yourself.

The greatness journey is about you taking the necessary steps to mentally accept that your journey will be a contest with only one participant. You aren't competing with anyone except the person within. No one else can determine your standard level except for you. To set the standard, growth and progression should be your focus. There should be continuous advancement with these two elements. Growth and progression are essential to the journey so you must do everything to stand out and set yourself apart.

If you are a giving person, this will be the one time I would encourage you to be selfish when

it comes to your standards. Consult with only those who have done what you are trying to do. Then set out to measure your standards by the progress you make. While your daily progress and productivity increases, so will your standards.

This is a platform where the playing field of life will not be level. All things will not be equal because of the difference that you embrace and embody as your new normal way of operating.

High Standards + Action
=
Progress towards your desired result

Choose your own level of greatness by setting your own standards.

Standards Gauge

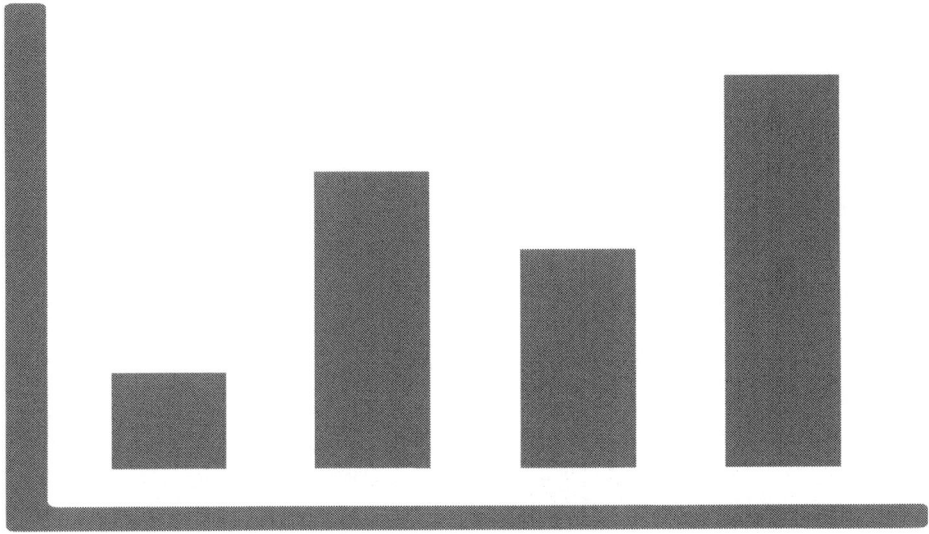

| Low Standards | Average Standards | High Standards |

Where do you stand?

The Word Says:

> Test everything. Hold on to the good.
> 1 Thessalonians 5:21

SUCCESS

"Successful people don't become that way overnight. What most people see at a glance is the result of goal setting, resilience, effort, having a positive attitude, being teachable, navigating challenges, executing action plans and having high-standards to go above and beyond so that the achievement of greatness is the result."
~Ramona Rogers

You have just read about the 8 elements that are essential to the Greatness process.

Just like a leprechaun looks for a pot of gold at the end of a rainbow, by following the GR8NESS formula, the pot of gold at the end of the Greatness formula is the reward of having a **SUCCESSFUL** life.

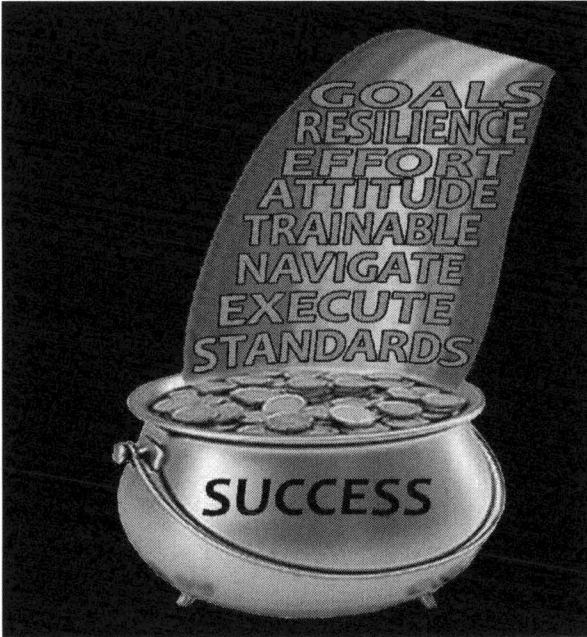

LIVE YOUR LIFE SO YOU CAN GET YOUR POT OF GOLD!

Success is a process!!

Success is a lot of little things done consistently day after day over a period of time.

Success is engineered from the inside out.

You must eradicate anything that is an enemy to you bringing out your GREATNESS. If you implement the formula daily in every aspect of your life, your level of GREATNESS will evolve.

Being average means, you are just like the general population. Being GREAT means, you have put in the work and time to set yourself apart.

Success means different things to different people. For this book and the formula that was laid out for you, that means you get to live your life on your own terms because you have gone the extra mile of arriving at the ultimate destination of becoming the GREAT person you were created to be. That accomplishment allows you to take advantage of opportunities and live out your hopes and dreams.

Success is making the decisions that you are going to become successful, then doing everything to move towards your desired result. That means doing everything well and excelling every step of the way.

The journey, with its element, forces you to evaluate from where you once were and then progress to the next stage or level. Anyone that has any level of Success has traveled down this road.

Take a moment to think about all the people who are viewed as successful.
They had to:

- ➢ Set **GOALS**
- ➢ Be **RESILIENT** when they had challenges
- ➢ Make an **EFFORT** to master new knowledge and skills
- ➢ Maintain a good **ATTITUDE**
- ➢ Be **TEACHABLE** and **TRAINABLE** at every level you progress to.
- ➢ **NAVIGATE** situations and obstacles that life will bring at every stage of your journey.
- ➢ **EXECUTE** your plans. You must **BE** action oriented in order to reach your Greatness destination.
- ➢ Set your **STANDARDS** high and work hard to meet and exceed them. You will end up in a class by yourself.

When you follow the Eight Elements that make up the GREATNESS Formula, you will get the GOLD Reward of being a SUCCESS.

The choice is yours. You have a formula to use. All you have to do now is decide that you deserve the gold that's at the end of the GREATNESS journey.

Your GREATNESS awaits.

Start your journey **TODAY!**

You are.... **GR8NESS IN THE MAKING!**

THE WORD SAYS:

> **"For I know the plans I have for you,"
> declares the Lord, "plans to prosper you
> and not harm you, plans to give you hope
> and a future."
> Jeremiah 29:11**

GREATNESS IN THE MAKING
CREED

(Recite Daily)

I Believe in myself!

I Believe in my ability!

I align my actions daily with the principles that promote greatness.

My journey will be filled with challenges and obstacles.

All are necessary so the Greatness in me can emerge.

Greatness is a process!

I'm committed to becoming the person I was created to be.

In the end, I will win!

I am... Greatness In The Making!

SUPPLEMENTAL TOOLS

Goal Setting

Daily Goals
1.
2.

Action Steps Goal 1
1.
2.

Action Steps Goal 2
1.
2.

Weekly Goals
1.
2.

Action Steps Goal 1
1.
2.

Action Steps Goal 2
1.
2.

Monthly Goals
1.
2.

Action Steps Goal 1
1.
2.

Action Steps Goal 2
1.
2.

3 months Goals
1.
2.
3.

Action Steps Goal 1
1.
2.
3.

Action Steps Goal 2
1.
2.
3.

Action Steps Goal 3
1.
2.
3.

6-month Goals
1.
2.
3.

Action Steps Goal 1
1.
2.
3.

Action Steps Goal 2
1.
2.
3.

Action Steps Goal 3
1.
2.
3.

1 Year Goals
1.
2.
3.

Action Steps Goal 1
1.
2.
3.

Action Steps Goal 2
1.
2.
3.

Action Steps Goal 3
1.
2.
3.

2 **Year Goals**

1.
2.
3.

Action Steps Goal 1

1.
2.
3.

Action Steps Goal 2

1.
2.
3.

Action Steps Goal 3

1.
2.
3.

Month
Year

Mon	Tues	Wed	Thurs	Fri	Sat	Sun

I AM...

GR8NESS IN THE MAKING

*NO GOAL WILL EVER BE REACHED UNLESS YOU PUT IN THE WORK TO REACH IT!

*GR8NESS IS A PROCESS!

*ALL YOUR ACTIONS SHOULD BE ALIGNED TO PROMOTE THE ELEMENTS OF GR8TNESS.!

ABOUT THE AUTHOR

Ramona Rogers is a Certified Executive Coach, Empowerment Speaker, Educator, Mentor, and Author.

She has spent the past 18 years positively impacting the lives of children, teens, and adults through her Coaching and Mentoring business, Ramona Rogers Enterprises.

She has heard people say for years that everyone has greatness inside of them. She believed that greatness was possible. Unfortunately, she had never came across a tool that marked out the day to day steps that would allow greatness to emerge in her life.

She has always helped individuals maneuver life's challenges to bring out the greatness within, but on June 22, 2017, God revealed the Greatness Formula to her.

This book, GR8NESS In The Making, was written to lay out the formula that will help anyone reach their level of Greatness.

The Eight elements will guide readers to create a blueprint to live by, so they can **Unlock the GREATNESS** they have inside and become the person they were created to be.

Made in the USA
Middletown, DE
30 December 2019